Great Quarterbacks

of Pro Football

Revised Edition

Great Quarterbacks
of Pro Football

Revised Edition

by STEVE GELMAN and
RITA GOLDEN GELMAN

SCHOLASTIC BOOK SERVICES

NEW YORK · TORONTO · LONDON · AUCKLAND · SYDNEY · TOKYO

Cover Photo: Mickey Palmer, Focus On Sports
Inside Photos: Courtesy Miami Dolphins, page 37; United
Press International, pages 17, 23, 25, 33, 41, 45, 67, 70, 73, 83,
113; Wide World Photos, frontispiece, pages 3, 6, 10, 29, 51,
57, 62, 80, 83, 91, 94, 98, 101, 106

ISBN: 0-590-30391-0

12 11 10 9 8 7 6 5 4   9/7 0 1 2 3/8
              Printed in the U.S.A.   11

Contents

For Jan and Mitchell

Pat Haden of the Los Angeles Rams. Doug France, a Ram offensive tackle, said, "Haden may be a young quarterback, but he has the poise of an old pro."

Pat Haden

Positive Thinker

"I know I'm going to spill this," you think as you walk to the table carrying a bowl of soup. The more you think about spilling the soup, the more nervous you get. And, of course, the more nervous you get, the better your chances are of spilling it.

Psychologists call it a "self-fulfilling prophesy." That's a lot of fancy words to say that if you convince yourself that something is going to happen, you sometimes make it happen.

Self-fulfilling prophesies work in good ways, too. Very often, if you think you are going to win, you work extra hard and you do win.

And that brings us to Pat Haden, quarterback for the Los Angeles Rams.

1

"You can do it, Pat," his two older brothers used to tell him when he was a little boy. "You can do it, Pat," they told him when his wobbly passes dropped to the ground. Then they would catch his passes for hours and hours as he kept improving.

"You can do it, Pat," they told him when he was stuck on a school project. And they would encourage him to work harder. They would answer his questions and push him to find his own answers. "You can do it, Pat. You can do it." You hear it often enough and you believe it.

"I ended up knowing that I could do anything I wanted to do," Pat remembered years later.

So Pat Haden, who thought he could do anything, drove into the Los Angeles Rams' training camp in the summer of 1976. He was 23 years old, but he could still hear that voice that said, "You can do it, Pat. You can do it."

Pat's blond hair flopped as he hopped out of his rented blue car and walked over to a bulletin board. A list of players was posted on the board. Next to each name was the number of the room each man would be living in during the days of training in Fullerton, California.

Pat looked over the list. There were 42 rookies on it —42 guys getting their first chance to be NFL players. Most of them had been stars of their college teams. All of them were hoping to become stars for the Rams. But

Haden loses the ball as San Diego Charger Leroy Jones hits him from behind. The Chargers recovered the fumble.

maybe six of them, if that many, would still be on the team when camp was over.

Like the other 41 rookies on the list, Pat had been a superstar. He had quarterbacked his California high school team to a championship. Then he had quarterbacked his college team, the University of Southern California, to three Rose Bowl games. In his last Rose Bowl game, millions of TV viewers had watched Pat throw a spectacular pass in the last seconds of the game for the winning touchdown. Then he had played one season in a new professional league called the World Football League, and had been a big star there, too.

Like the other 41 rookies on the list, Pat had proven himself on the football field, and the Rams had drafted him. Now, here he was, trying out for a National Football League team that already had two fine veteran quarterbacks — Ron Jaworski and James Harris. Pat seemed to have no chance of beating them out. Experts agreed that it took several years for a young man to become an effective quarterback in the National Football League. But Pat knew better. ("You can do it, Pat. You can do it.")

True, he was small. Only 5-10½.

True, he was light. Only 173 pounds.

True, he had a lot to learn. He knew all that.

But deep inside, Pat had a feeling that something good was going to happen to him. "I don't know *what*," he wrote in his diary. "Maybe somebody will get traded. But good things always happen to me. I've come to expect them."

("You can do it, Pat. You can do it.")

The feeling had always been there. And good things *were* always happening to him. Pat says he's just lucky. He says he was lucky in high school because he had such terrific athletes on his team: "In high school I fell in with a tremendous receiver like John McKay, Jr., [who went into pro ball with Tampa Bay] and I was surrounded by tremendous athletes. We won a championship."

He says he was lucky in college because USC had such a good team: "I came into USC just at the right time and we won two national championships with some extremely talented people around me."

But luck doesn't happen so consistently. There's something more than luck going on when a person is a consistent winner.

So there Pat was, at the Rams' training camp, and something inside him told him he was going to beat out the other rookie quarterbacks for the number three spot. And something else told him he was going to end up number one.

If he had shared his feelings with almost anyone who knew anything about football, they'd all have said he was crazy. What about James Harris? What about Ron Jaworski? They were fine quarterbacks and they had pro experience.

Six points! Pat Haden jumps for joy after scoring a stand-up touchdown from the 7-yard line.

But Pat didn't listen to anybody else. And he worked as though he were number one. He practiced as though the whole team depended on him. He learned the playbook and studied defenses as though the future of the Rams depended on Pat Haden.

And then it happened. Just two weeks before the first game of the season, James Harris, number one quarterback, broke his thumb. "Be ready," they told Pat. "You're number two now."

Pat, of course, was ready even before they told him to be ready.

The opening game was in Atlanta, Georgia. It was a beautiful sunny day. Early in the third quarter, with the Rams winning 12-7, Ron Jaworski walked to the bench rubbing his arm. "Feels numb," he said. Ron went in for one more play, but he couldn't handle the ball. "I can't feel a thing in my arm," he said.

So out ran rookie Pat Haden. Like an experienced pro, he took over the team. After a few minutes, Pat had the ball on the Atlanta 47. The coach sent in a running play and Pat called it in the huddle. But as the Atlanta defense lined up, Pat noticed a change in their formation. The planned play wouldn't work. So Pat called a different play. A pass play. He called the new signals, faded back, and threw the ball 56 yards in the air. Ron Jessie of the Rams caught it in the end zone. Touchdown! Pat's first pass in the NFL was a touchdown.

First time out...all those people...the whole team counting on him. Pressure is the thing that usually gets the rookies. But pressure didn't bother Pat a bit. "He's so cool," said one of the Rams' coaches.

He never doubted himself. So he came through.

The injuries to Harris and Jaworski gave Pat a chance to show his stuff. But before the season ended, even though the two veterans were healthy and back again playing, Pat was the number one quarterback. And he took the Rams to the Western Division Championship of the league's National Football Conference.

Was it luck? Was it because he had a terrific team? Or was it something that Pat Haden did or said, or something about the way he quarterbacked, that made his season so successful? Doug France, the big Ram offensive tackle, tried to explain it to a newspaper columnist.

"Haden may be a young quarterback," France said, "but he has the poise of an old pro, and he knows how to say the right things at the right time. Nobody ever really pays much attention to the offensive line, unless it makes mistakes, but Haden makes his line feel good. He'll say, 'Way to go, line,' after he completes a pass or one of the running backs makes a gain.

"Or he'll say, 'You're doing fine, we'll get 'em next time,' if the play doesn't go so well. The point is that Haden always says something to make his line personnel feel good. Today, when McCutcheon made a real good gain, Haden came up to me and said, 'Thanks for opening that big hole!' Man, I felt ten feet high. Imagine that kid thanking me for opening a hole! That's my job, but Haden made me feel like I had just done something extra special. You want to break your neck for a guy like that."

So maybe it wasn't luck after all. Maybe it was Pat Haden.

Oh, sure, sometimes luck was involved. Like back in high school, when Pat deliberately threw the ball out of bounds because his receiver was covered. And the wind blew the football right back onto the field and into the hands of his receiver. That was luck.

But it isn't luck when Pat brings out the best in a team. When he comes in and prods them and pushes them and suddenly they begin playing like champs.

Sometimes it takes a while, though, before people are really convinced that someone like Pat is really all that good, that his victories are due to skill and confidence and a very special way of leading people. The Rams' coaches and owner, for example, didn't really believe in him—not even after his great rookie season. After all, he was such a little guy for an NFL quarterback. And he had so little pro experience. And his arm wasn't nearly as strong as those of other pro passers.

So, for the next season, 1977, the Rams signed superstar Joe Namath, who hadn't been doing well lately, but once had been the absolutely best quarterback in the world. Pat dropped back to number two

Haden gained a few yards on this "keeper" play. Lunging toward him is Tom Myers (37) of the New Orleans Saints.

again. "We're going with Joe because of his experience," said coach Chuck Knox.

But Joe got hurt and couldn't come through. So they gave the job back to Pat. Once again he led the Los Angeles Rams to the NFC Western Division championship. And a lot of people felt he was going to take the Rams even further—all the way to the Super Bowl. Pat thought so, too. But during the first playoff game, it rained and the field became muddy. The Rams had trouble moving in the mud. Their offense fell apart. For the first time all season, Pat did not play well. And the Minnesota Vikings upset them.

A few days after the season, Pat and his wife, Cindy, went to England. During Pat's senior year in college he had applied for a Rhodes Scholarship—a special, high honor which allows a handful of young U.S. students to study for two years at Oxford University in England.

Pat had written on his application: "I get good grades, but I work hard...I have been so concerned with getting good grades and so occupied with football that I have not done enough to enrich my intellect...I would like to have the free time and a free mind to write poetry, to study contemporary literature, and to look into other things I enjoy, like music..."

Pat had won a Rhodes Scholarship. He had spent time at Oxford after college and, again, after his rookie year with the Rams. Now, after the 1977 season, Pat was returning for his final months at Oxford. "It's really different over there," he told a reporter from *The Sporting News*. "No pressure, no commotion, no boos. I have a lot of free time to just sit down and do a lot of thinking and a lot of reading. I really like it for the first couple of months, but I get tired of it after a while. I begin missing the camaraderie you find on a football team, the thrill of playing in front of a large crowd and doing something that I do well. I feel like I'm missing part of my life."

Pat said he planned to become a lawyer. But before that, he said, he hoped to quarterback the Rams to Super Bowl victory.

There were still a lot of doubters, a lot of people who didn't think he had the talent to do it.

"He doesn't have such a great arm," they kept saying. "Good, but not spectacular."

"He doesn't have terrific speed," they would say. "Fast, but not extraordinary."

"He doesn't even have the best football head in the business," they would say. "There are quarterbacks who can spot defenses better and make quicker adjustments."

"And he's short and light and inexperienced. So why should you expect so much of him?"

What his critics didn't understand was that Pat Haden is a winner. Throughout his life, he's had a voice that keeps telling him, "You can do it, Pat. You can do it."

So he does.

Pro Football Passing Record of:

Patrick Capper Haden

Birthday: Jan. 23, 1953   Height: 5-11   Weight: 182

Team: Los Angeles Rams (1976-   )

Nickname: Pat

Year	Passes Thrown	Passes Completed	Percent	Average Gain	Total Yards	Touch-downs	Inter-ceptions
1976	105	60	57.1	8.53	896	8	4
1977	216	122	56.5	7.18	1551	11	6

Roger Staubach

Running Cowboy

Question: What is an ostrich with four eyes?
Answer: Roger Staubach.

Well, maybe he's not an ostrich. Okay, he doesn't have four eyes. But *Time* Magazine once said that with his long, stilt-like legs, Roger looked like an ostrich. And, according to the magazine, "Opposing coaches swear that Roger has eyes in the back of his head."

From the time he was a boy, coaches said things like that about Roger because he always seemed to know what was going on behind him as well as in front of him. And he had a knack for doing the unexpected. When Roger lined up at quarterback, took the ball from the center, and rolled around to the right, anything could happen. "At that point," said one coach, "nobody knows what he's going to do except Staubach and God."

One season, when he was a college quarterback, Roger did a lot of running with the ball. He scrambled around tacklers. He found holes in the line and shot through them. He wove in and out of players to score touchdowns.

During that season, one team figured out how to beat him. All they had to do was stop his running game. They drilled their defense for weeks and their plan worked. They stopped his running. But Roger threw 22 passes, completed 17 of them, and beat the team, 51-7.

"The only way to beat him," said one coach, "would be to let the air out of the football."

By then, Roger was a tall, powerful young man, six feet, three inches and 195 pounds. But he hadn't forgotten the days when he was so small and slight that his parents wouldn't allow him to play tackle football.

That had happened when Roger was growing up in Cincinnati, Ohio. He'd had to settle for touch football until he was in seventh grade. Then he was allowed to join a real football team at the St. John's Boys Club. Roger finally got to the thing he loved best — running with a football. He played halfback for two years.

When Roger joined the Purcell High School team as a freshman, he played halfback and end. But when he returned the next year, his coach told him, "You're going to be a quarterback this season."

Roger was upset, nearly in tears. He went home and told his parents, "I don't want to play quarterback. I love to run with the ball, and on this team the quarterback isn't allowed to run very much."

But Roger soon discovered that throwing could be as exciting as running. And the coach let him run a lot, too. For three years, Roger ran and passed for his high-school team, and he was an outstanding quarterback.

At the end of his senior year, more than 30 colleges offered him scholarships.

Roger studied the offers. Finally, he decided he wanted to attend the U.S. Naval Academy at Annapolis, Maryland. But before he could go there, he had to take an entrance exam. And he flunked it.

Roger could go to a different school, or he could attend a junior college for a year, study hard, and take the exam again. He decided to spend a year at junior college. He worked hard and studied long hours. The next time he took the test, he passed.

When Roger entered the Naval Academy in 1961, he joined the freshman football team — the "plebe" team. At the Academy, the freshmen are called "plebes" and they spend a lot of time taking orders from the older students. It's a tradition that the lowly "plebes" have to serve their elders.

One day, the "plebe" football team played the varsity team. The upperclassmen all knew what to expect — the freshmen would stumble and fumble all over the field, and the varsity would run all over them.

The first time Roger got the ball, he ran — all around the upperclassmen and across the goal line for a touchdown.

Wayne Hardin, the varsity coach, shook his head. "He was just lucky," Hardin said to himself. "Just lucky."

But luck had nothing to do with it. Hardin found that

The Marvelous Middie—
Roger Staubach as mid-
shipman at Annapolis.

Getting into tip top shape.
Staubach, known as the
"Navy Destroyer," won
the Heisman trophy for
outstanding performance
in college football.

out the next year when Roger played on the varsity team.

On the varsity, Roger watched the first few games from the bench — waiting for his chance. He got it in a game against Cornell. The score was 0-0 when Hardin signaled for Staubach to go in. In 23 minutes, Roger ran for two touchdowns and passed for one. Navy won the game easily.

Roger's performance fired up the school. The big game was coming—Army (the U.S. Military Academy) vs. Navy (the U.S. Naval Academy). It was an old rivalry and Army had a good team.

Until the Cornell game, Navy's hopes for beating Army were slight. But now the whole Navy campus was confident. No one could stop Roger, not even Army.

The students waved and yelled when they saw him on campus. They couldn't stop talking about their new young star. They even made a huge banner that read "Home of Roger Staubach."

Roger didn't let them down. He blitzed Army, 34-14.

Roger didn't spend all his time playing football, of course. He was a hard-working student. And he was serious, gentle, and religious. One of the officers at the Naval Academy once told a reporter that "for four years at the Academy, Roger was the altar boy at daily Mass."

There were moments of fun, too. Final exam week was a tense time in the dormitory, where the students lived. People barely talked to each other. They just buried their heads in books. One day, two of Roger's teammates were studying. Roger sneaked into their room and threw a water bomb at them. They were soaked.

One of them raced to Roger's room with a glass of water. He threw open the door, but Roger was waiting for him — in a raincoat.

In 1963, Roger won the Heisman Trophy, which is awarded each season to the best college football player in the nation. But unlike most college stars who go on to play for a pro team, Roger could not. When a student graduates from the U.S. Naval Academy, he is required to serve four years in the Navy.

Before Roger left school to become an officer, the Dallas Cowboys got in touch with him. They knew he could not play for them for four years. And after that, he might choose to stay in the Navy. But they were willing to take a gamble. They agreed to pay Roger $5,000 a year for the four years he would be in the Navy. Even if he decided to stay in the Navy and never play pro football, he could keep the money. They hoped, of course, that at the end of four years, Roger would choose to play ball with them rather than make the Navy his career.

Roger spent a year in the United States with the Navy, then two years in Vietnam. In 1968, when he returned again to the U.S., he still had to serve one more year as a Naval officer. But the Navy gave him a two-week leave so he could spend some time at training camp with the Cowboys.

Roger was nervous when he left for the training camp. He knew this was it! After this trip, he would either be a pro player with the Cowboys or he'd remain in the Navy.

He and his wife, Marianne, had spent many hours talking about the decision. They liked Navy life, but Roger also loved football. And the real question in his head as he walked into camp was: "Do I still have what it takes? Am I good enough to make it after three years?"

He was. The Cowboy coaches were pleased with his passing and running. And a year later, when he was discharged from the Navy, Roger reported to the Cowboys with a chance of becoming their number two quarterback.

He trained hard. When the rest of the Cowboys finished their day's work and left the field to shower, relax, and go home, Roger would convince a few teammates to stay out on the field with him and catch passes. Often, Bob Belden, another young quarterback, would remain on the field, too. They would take turns passing to the receivers.

When the last receiver would drag himself off the field, Roger and Bob would begin to clown around. Roger would run down the sidelines, leaping in the air like an antelope and howling, "Hee-yah." Bob would throw him a long pass. Still leaping and howling, Roger would catch the ball on his fingertips and run full speed up a hill, down a hill, and into the locker room a half mile away!

When training camp ended, Roger had won the job as the number two quarterback. Then he sat on the bench for two seasons. He played only once in a while but he learned a lot about pro football. And in 1971, Roger's third pro season, coach Tom Landry decided that Roger was now as good as the team's top quarterback, Craig Morton.

Only Landry couldn't decide which of them was better. So he had them take turns playing quarterback. Roger felt under constant pressure. He felt that every move he made was being judged. More than anything, he wanted to prove that he should be number one. He felt that every second he spent on the field was important.

Once when it was Roger's turn to start the next game, a reporter noticed a huge bruise on one of Roger's legs. "It was about the size of an eggplant, yellow and green around the edges," the reporter said later.

The reporter asked Roger about the bruise.

"A pulled muscle," Roger said. "but that isn't going to keep me from playing Sunday. I guarantee you that. Not after I've come this far."

Roger picked up a lot of bruises as the 1971 season rolled on. In one game, everyone watched the ball as Roger threw a pass. When the play was over, Roger was on the ground, knocked out, and he had to leave the game. Because all eyes had been on the ball, no one knew what had happened to him.

When the movies of the game were shown, the Cowboys discovered that a player on the other team had apparently clobbered Roger with his forearm on purpose.

"I'd like to get him alone a few minutes in a back alley somewhere," Roger said.

"But he's six-four and weighs 250," someone said. "What would you do with him in a back alley?"

"Listen," said Roger, "I've got four years of hand-to-hand combat I never got to use."

People were surprised at that burst of anger because Roger was always so calm, such a gentleman on and off the field. But pressure gets to everyone sometimes, and the Cowboys were under great strain. They had won four games and had lost three. At that rate, they'd never make it to the Super Bowl. And they wanted to, badly, because they had played in the Super Bowl the previous year and lost.

People were saying the Cowboys would never be champions of pro football because they were never able to play their best when it counted most. Some people, on and off the team, felt that Landry should make a decision between Staubach and Morton. With a strong quarterback as leader, the Cowboys could prove that they were winners.

It was a happy day for Roger when Coach Landry

finally announced that no longer would his two quarterbacks take turns. From now on, the Cowboys' quarterback would be Roger Staubach.

"It's fantastic," Roger said. "Now if I make a few mistakes, I'll still be in there. I won't be walking a tightrope anymore. This way I'll come through a winner."

And he did. He led the Cowboys to seven straight victories during the rest of the season, then to two more victories in the playoffs. And now the Cowboys were again in the Super Bowl.

Dallas coach Tom Landry with his No. 1 quarterback, Roger Staubach.

The morning of Super Bowl VI, a man was talking to Commodore Paul Borden of the U.S. Navy. Borden had been at the Naval Academy when Roger was there.

"Did it ever occur to you, Commodore," the man said, "that this is really Staubach's first Super Bowl? If any Cowboy is going to feel the pressure, it's him."

The commodore shook his head. "This game is a big game," he said. "But I'm not sure how much bigger it is in comparison to the Army-Navy games when Roger was so much younger. Every midshipman, every officer — why, every admiral in the fleet — they were all on Roger's shoulders. But he thrives on pressure. He seems to respond to it perfectly."

Whether it was pressure or something else, Roger played a magnificent game. He faked with perfection. He passed with precision. And he ran through the Miami Dolphins' defense with the speed of a sprinter and the balance of a dancer. The final score was Dallas — 24, Miami — 3. And the man chosen as the game's Most Valuable Player was Roger Staubach.

All through the season, Roger told people he had been doing "a lot of weight lifting to keep in shape. At the end of the weight lifting each day, no matter how tired I was, I always said, 'Let's lift one more for the Super Bowl.'"

And now, that extra effort had clearly paid off.

Roger continued to play for the Cowboys for many more years, and brought them many more victories. In January, 1978 Staubach led the Cowboys to another

Running Cowboy in action: Vikings' Jim Marshall pounds after a racing Roger.

great Super Bowl win over the Denver Broncos. But even after his tenth year with the Dallas team, nothing seemed as important to Roger as winning Super Bowl VI. In his first season as a starting pro quarterback, he had led his team to the championship of all pro football.

Pro Football Passing Record of:

Roger Staubach

Birthday: Feb. 5, 1945   Height: 6-3   Weight: 195
Team: Dallas Cowboys (1969–   )

Year	Passes Thrown	Passes Completed	Percent	Average Gain	Total Yards	Touch-downs	Inter-ceptions
1969	47	23	48.9	8.96	421	1	2
1970	82	44	53.7	6.61	542	2	8
1971	211	126	59.7	8.92	1882	15	4
1972	20	9	45.0	4.90	98	0	2
1973	286	179	62.6	8.49	2428	23	15
1974	360	190	52.8	7.09	2552	11	15
1975	348	198	56.9	7.66	2666	17	16
1976	369	208	56.4	7.36	2715	14	11
1977	361	210	58.2	7.26	2620	18	9

In 1971 and 1973, Staubach led the NFL in average gain per pass.

In 1973, he led the NFL in touchdown passes.

Ken Stabler

Ouch to Whammo

It wasn't one of those "Zap! Pow! Whammo!" beginnings. You know, the kind where the new quarterback runs out on the field, throws for a bunch of touchdowns, and becomes an instant hero. No, it wasn't like that at all. Ken Stabler's pro football career had more of an "Ouch! Oops! Snore!" beginning. And that "beginning" went on for *five years*! Then...

But to start with, when Ken joined the Oakland Raiders as a rookie in 1968, one of the first things he did was have a physical examination. Bad knee, said the doctor. Needs rest. Before Ken had even thrown a practice pass, he was out for the season. *Ouch*!

In 1969, Ken reported to training camp, knee healed.

But this time he had personal problems. After just a few days of practice, he left camp to try to work them out. He didn't come back for the rest of the season. *Oops!*

In 1970, 1971, and 1972, Ken played with the team. (Or not exactly *play*. Mostly, he sat on the bench.) *Snore!*

"All I want is a chance," Ken kept saying. "It's a frustrating thing, not playing when you think you should be playing. It's the hardest thing I've gone through since being in pro football."

As Ken sat through those seasons, growing very unhappy, he had many long talks with a teammate named George Blanda. George had been playing pro football for more than 20 years. He was a quarterback himself and he knew how badly Ken felt. But he also knew that Ken was a good player and would someday get a chance.

"Stay around, take care of yourself, and be ready," George kept telling Ken. "That's the best thing for you."

Ken listened.

It was after the third game of the 1973 season that Ken finally got his chance. Oakland had won one game and lost two. Coach John Madden knew it was time to make some changes. The coach turned over the quarterback job to Ken for the rest of the season.

Ken was *spectacular*! In fact, in one game, against

Ken Stabler, sensational southpaw quarterback for Oakland Raiders.

the Baltimore Colts, he threw 29 passes and completed 25 of them. His passing percentage for that game was 86.2 percent, a National Football League record. At the end of the season, Oakland had won nine games and lost only three with Ken at quarterback. A headline in a local newspaper read, "Stabler took over, Raiders took off."

The Oakland fans were excited about their new star. Where had he been the past three years? The answer, of course, was — on the bench.

Until he joined the Oakland Raiders, Ken had never sat on the bench. In Foley, Alabama, where Ken was born and grew up, he starred in basketball, baseball, and football for the town high school. Playing for the Foley High football team as a freshman, Ken ran back one punt 70 yards for a touchdown. But he zigged and zagged from side to side so much to elude tacklers he actually ran about 300 yards before he made it over the goal line. "Boy," said the coach, "you ran just like a snake!"

From then on, Ken's nickname was "Snake."

Ken's father was the head of the service department at the Chevrolet agency in Foley. Ken grew up knowing how to take apart all those things under a car's hood, and when he was old enough he bought his own hot rods and motorcycles. "I love speed," he said many years later. "Besides fast cars and motorcycles, I like to water ski."

From Foley High, Ken went to the University of Alabama. He played quarterback there and led his team to two bowl games. During his last two years as Alabama's quarterback, the team won 19 games, lost only two, and tied one.

Ken's coach at Alabama was very proud of him. So proud that he said, "Ken Stabler is the best passer I've ever had."

People were very surprised when he said that. The coach, you see, was Bear Bryant. And only a few years earlier, Bear had been the coach of Joe Namath.

Ken was surprised, too. When a reporter asked him how he felt about Bear's praise, Ken got a shy smile on his round, handsome face. Then he looked at the man through his clear blue eyes. "Aw, Bear just says things like that," Ken said. "Joe's the best passer there is."

Amazingly, the pro football teams didn't seem very interested in Ken. There were two reasons. First, Ken was not only a football star, he was also an excellent baseball player. The Houston Astros wanted him to pitch for them, and the pro football teams thought he was more interested in baseball than in football. Second, Ken was lefthanded, and very few lefthanded quarterbacks had ever made it in pro football. The ball spins differently when it is thrown by a lefty. A lot of pro coaches were worried that their pass receivers would have trouble catching Ken's passes.

But Ken really did like football better than baseball,

and he was confident he could succeed even though he was a lefty. After all, the receivers at Alabama had caught his passes. He turned down the offer from the Astros, joined the Oakland Raiders, and once he got his chance he became a star.

In 1973, the first year that he was Oakland's starting quarterback, Ken led the team to the championship of their division. He also led the National Football League in percent of passes completed.

In 1974, his second season as starting quarterback, Ken again led the Raiders to the division championship. He threw more touchdown passes than anyone else in the National Football League. And he was picked as the Player of the Year in the American Football Conference.

Ken also provided pro football fans with one of the biggest thrills of the 1974 season. In the last few seconds of their playoff game against the Miami Dolphins, the Raiders were losing. They had the ball deep in Miami territory with time for only one more play. A field goal wouldn't be enough. They needed a touchdown to win. And Ken Stabler was the man who had to get it for them.

Ken called for a pass play. Then he faded back, looking into the end zone. The Dolphin pass rushers charged, forced him to the side, and leaped at him. Down he went, falling toward the ground. Suddenly, an instant before he hit the grass, he flung the football. He

"Ken the Snake," nicknamed for his zigzag running pattern, about to pass. "The best passer I've ever had," Bear Bryant, his college coach, once said.

had spotted an Oakland player in the end zone, and fired the ball at him.

Now Ken was flat on the ground. And the ball was in the air. He heard an enormous wild cheer. The ball had been caught. Oakland had won.

Sadly for Ken, Oakland lost the next game and did not make it to the Super Bowl. Nor did they make it the year after that.

Then, in 1976, Ken had his greatest season ever. He led Oakland to the championship of its division, to two playoff victories, and to the Super Bowl. In the Super Bowl, Ken completed 12 passes for 180 yards and brought Oakland a 32-14 victory over the Minnesota Vikings. For the first time ever, the Oakland Raiders were the champions of all pro football. And Ken had done it for them.

He certainly had a lot to be proud of. He had never given up, not in all those years of injuries and personal problems and sitting on the bench. He had waited for an opportunity to prove himself. And when it finally came, he had made the most of it. Whammo!

Pro Football Passing Record of:

Kenneth Michael Stabler

Birthday: Dec. 25, 1945   Height: 6-3   Weight: 215

Team: Oakland Raiders (1970-   )

Nicknames: Ken, Snake

Year	Passes Thrown	Passes Completed	Percent	Average Gain	Total Yards	Touch-downs	Inter-ceptions
1970	7	2	28.6	7.43	52	0	1
1971	48	24	50.0	5.58	268	1	4
1972	74	44	59.5	7.08	524	4	3
1973	260	163	62.7	7.68	1997	14	10
1974	310	178	57.4	7.96	2469	26	12
1975	293	171	58.4	7.84	2296	16	24
1976	291	194	66.7	9.41	2737	27	17
1977	294	169	57.5	7.40	2176	20	20

In 1973 and 1976, Stabler led the NFL in percent of passes completed.

In 1974 and 1976, he led the NFL in touchdown passes.

In 1976 he led the NFL in average gain per pass.

Bob Griese

Cool Dolphin

A man and woman stood at the Miami airport with suitcases in their hands. They were Bob Griese's aunt and uncle from Indiana. They had come to Miami to visit their nephew who played quarterback for the Miami Dolphins. Bob was supposed to pick them up and take them to his house.

Instead, a big limousine pulled up in front of them. A uniformed chauffeur sat at the wheel. A fancy-dressed butler sat next to him. Both men had huge black walrus mustaches.

"We will drive you to Mr. Griese's home," said the butler.

Bob's aunt and uncle couldn't believe it. They were plain people from Indiana. Certainly Bob didn't have to be fancy with them.

Bob Griese poses for camera. He led Miami Dolphins to Super Bowl 3 times and to victory there twice.

They climbed in, and the chauffeur turned around. He had sparkling blue eyes, reddish blond hair, and there was something familiar about the face surrounding the mustache. Suddenly, the aunt and uncle recognized their nephew Bob.

Bob and a friend were playing a practical joke. Bob had rented the car and the uniforms. And he and his friend had bought the mustaches.

Bob enjoyed practical jokes. They made him laugh—and they made other people laugh. But he didn't pull practical jokes very often. Most of the time he was serious. Serious and quiet.

"I've always been quiet," Bob said, soon after he became a Miami Dolphin. "I'd just as soon be off by myself as be with a big group."

Bob spent a lot of time by himself in his first years with the Dolphins. While the other players watched TV or relaxed with each other, Bob usually sat alone in his hotel room. He spent many of those quiet hours studying his football plays, or watching movies of football games, or thinking about what the coaches had told him. There were so many things to study about football. So much to learn.

Bob had always been willing to spend a lot of time learning football. Back when he was a boy, in fact, he had taught himself the game. In his hometown, Evansville, Indiana, there were Little League baseball teams and there were basketball teams for young boys. But no football teams.

"We learned on our own," Bob once recalled. "Kids my age—nine, ten, eleven, twelve years old. We never had a regular field.

"I remember playing in the side yard of our house, which was very close to the house next door. It wasn't easy to get around anybody and run for a score because the field was too narrow. So the games were made up of throwing. Almost every play was a pass, which forced me to perfect my passing. Besides, runs were dangerous. The bricks on the house next door were very rough and coarse. If you got too close, you could scrape your face badly. Too close to my house and you might take a fall on a concrete sidewalk that ran the length of the field."

Bob was the youngest boy in his group. "Being the smallest, I took more punishment than anyone else. But later, when I began playing with kids my own age, the lessons I learned from older kids put me a step ahead—a little better runner, a little better passer, a little better blocker."

When Bob was 12 years old, his father died. Bob missed his father terribly. His whole life had changed. "My father's death had a big effect on me," Bob told a reporter, years later. "I listened more attentively than most boys to what coaches told me because I didn't have a father. Coaches were a kind of substitute father for me."

At Rex Mundi High School in Evansville, Bob worked very hard for the football coach. And for two straight years Bob was selected as the best high-school quarterback in the state of Indiana.

When he arrived at Purdue University in 1963, Bob was a side-arm passer. His throws were wobbly. Purdue's assistant coach, Bob DeMoss, taught him how to throw overhand. DeMoss also gave Bob lessons on how to release his passes quickly, before tacklers could swarm him.

In his sophomore season at Purdue, Bob was the number one quarterback. He was also the team's best kicker. In his very first game, he kicked a 36-yard field goal and ran for two touchdowns. He also kicked two extra points. Purdue won, 17-0. Bob had scored every single point.

The next season, Bob was at quarterback when Purdue played Notre Dame. The Notre Dame team was expected to win easily. But Bob completed 19 of 22 passes, and Purdue upset Notre Dame, 25-21. After the game Notre Dame's coach, Ara Parseghian, couldn't stop talking about Bob. "Griese's was the greatest performance I have ever seen," Parseghian said.

In his senior year, Bob led Purdue to the Rose Bowl. By then, pro scouts were watching him in every game. And when Purdue won the Rose Bowl game, 14-13, Joe Thomas—the director of player personnel for the Miami Dolphins—went down to the locker room to meet Bob.

"I had been watching him play since he was a sophomore," Thomas told reporters later, "but this was the first time I had talked to him. You could see he was going to be a good one—quick feet, quick arm—and he had that fluid way of moving, like a thoroughbred. With a quarterback, though, you want to get an impression of his personality and intelligence. He was very wide-eyed and alert, and he had a way of looking straight at you that I liked."

A few weeks later, Bob flew to Hawaii to play in the Hula Bowl all-star game. While there Bob and his teammate, George Catavalos, decided to go body surfing. But there was a fierce undertow.

"George and I went out about 10 yards," Bob remembered afterward, "and the next thing we knew, we

Bob watches his tennis partner, Chris Evert, return a shot.

were out 40 yards. George started yelling and I went over to grab him and we were both in trouble. I started yelling, too. We nearly drowned. But, finally, five or six Hawaiians swam out and pulled us in as easy as if they were just strolling around."

When Bob returned from Hawaii, he learned that the Dolphins had picked him as their first choice in the pro football draft. He reported to them for the 1967 season and became the number two quarterback. But in the first game, the number one quarterback hurt his ankle. Bob came in, completed 12 of 19 passes, and led Miami to a 35-21 win.

After that, though, the Dolphins didn't win many games. For three seasons Bob played very well, but in all that time the Dolphins won only 11 games.

Then, in 1970, Don Shula took over as head coach. It took him only two seasons to turn the Dolphins into the champions of the American Football Conference.

The Dolphins played in the Super Bowl after winning their first American Football Conference championship, and they lost to the Dallas Cowboys. The next season, though, the Dolphins won every single game they played. No National Football League team had ever before gone through a season undefeated, but the Dolphins did it. They won 17 straight games, including the Super Bowl against the Washington Redskins in 1973. And in the Super Bowl, Bob Griese was the star of their offense. He threw a touchdown pass to Howard

Twilley and he set up another touchdown with a pass to Jim Mandich. Those two touchdowns were all the Dolphins needed. They won the Super Bowl, 14-7.

The next season Bob and the Dolphins were again champions. This time they played the Minnesota Vikings in the Super Bowl, and beat them, 24-7. The very first time the Dolphins got the ball, Bob led them in for a touchdown. After that, it was a slaughter. The Vikings never had a chance.

After that second Super Bowl victory, most people agreed that Bob had become the top quarterback in pro football. Before him, Joe Namath had been the very best. And before that, it had been Bart Starr and Johnny Unitas. Now, for a while anyway, it was Bob's turn.

The Dolphins slumped right after that second Super Bowl victory, but Bob didn't. He had two fine seasons in a row, particularly 1975, when he gained an average of 8.86 yards with each of his passes, tops in the NFL. And the Dolphins began counting on him more than ever. They lost a lot of their star runners in the years following the Super Bowl victories, including the man who was then the best fullback in the game, Larry Csonka. Bob's passing therefore became even more important than before.

But in 1976 Bob had some problems. Suddenly he wasn't able to pick out his receivers as well as in the past. He became very worried. "I started to notice some double vision," he said later. "And some dizziness. I didn't know what was wrong."

The problem was that he needed eyeglasses. And when he got them Bob was as good as ever. With his new glasses, Bob threw pinpoint passes all through the 1977 season. Under the National Football League's official rating system, which judges quarterbacks on a combination of passing statistics, Bob was the top passer in pro football in 1977, with Roger Staubach, Pat Haden, Craig Morton, and Bert Jones following him in that order. And Bob's Dolphins had a 10-4 record, their best since the Super Bowl years.

When people talked about Bob's talent, they talked about his strong, accurate passing. But probably the most outstanding part of Bob's game was his amazing ability to know what the other team was going to do. That is called "reading defenses." And it's a lot like being a detective.

Is the other team going to shift at the last moment to prevent a pass, leaving a hole open for a runner? Is it going to stack its players against a run, leaving a pass receiver free? Is it going to leave its linebackers in their regular positions to defend against runs and short passes? Or is it going to send its linebackers shooting in at the quarterback on a "blitz"? A quarterback has to figure all that out.

Almost from the time he broke into pro football, Bob had a knack for reading defenses. As he took his place at

Griese loses his famous cool in the heat of the game.

the line of scrimmage, his blue eyes would peer through his helmet-cage, scanning the other team. One move by an opponent, one glance, one step would give Bob clues as to what the defensive team's strategy was.

"I don't know how he does it," said one of his opponents, Pete Richardson of Buffalo. "He always seems to know which way I am going. I'll take two steps to the right when he's calling signals, but it's like he is looking into my head and he knows I'm going to come back those two steps before the ball is snapped. And on the blitz, he's really something. He always seems to know when you're blitzing."

Even Bob himself once said, "It's a real funny thing. I mean, sometimes you can look into their eyes and you can *tell* they're blitzing."

But it wasn't really magic. Bob was so good at reading defenses because he worked hard and had a brilliant understanding of the game. He spent hours studying movies of every team the Dolphins played—hours watching for giveaway motions before certain plays. Did that linebacker move a little closer to the line of scrimmage before he blitzed? Bob would run the film over and over and look carefully. Did the defensive back glance across the field at the man he was going to cover? Bob would watch the films again and again, looking for clues.

Bob was also a calm and careful quarterback. In a game he never got excited. Even his teammates watched with wonder as Bob stayed cool in every situation. They began to ask each other if anything, at any time, could make Bob lose his cool.

One day during training camp, Bob was in his room with Jack Clancy, a teammate. Jack leaned over to fix the stereo, glanced under the bed and yelled, "Bob, what's that thing?"

"I went over there," Bob later recalled, "looked under the bed and there was one of those tanklike animals—you know, about two feet long with armor shell. Well, I yelled and Jack yelled and we almost knocked over each other trying to get through the door. I went down the hall yelling, 'Hey! There's an animal in our room! Somebody come here!' "

Two of the Dolphins came out their room, laughing. One of them went in, picked up the "ferocious animal" by its tail, and went off to scare someone else. It was only a harmless armadillo. Bob had been the victim of a practical joke. And his teammates had succeeded in doing something that Dolphin opponents had never been able to do. Finally, somebody had made Bob Griese lose his cool.

Pro Football Passing Record of:

Robert Allen Griese

Birthday: Feb. 3, 1945   Height: 6-1   Weight: 190

Team: Miami Dolphins (1967-   )

Nickname: Bob

Year	Passes Thrown	Passes Completed	Percent	Average Gain	Total Yards	Touch-downs	Inter-ceptions
1967	331	166	50.2	6.06	2005	15	18
1968	355	186	52.4	6.97	2473	21	16
1969	252	121	48.0	6.73	1695	10	16
1970	245	142	58.0	8.24	2019	12	17
1971	263	145	55.1	7.94	2089	19	9
1972	97	53	54.6	6.58	638	4	4
1973	218	116	53.2	6.52	1422	17	8
1974	253	152	60.1	7.78	1968	16	15
1975	191	118	61.8	8.86	1693	14	13
1976	272	162	59.6	7.71	2097	11	12
1977	307	180	58.6	7.34	2252	22	13

In 1975, Bob led the NFL in average gain per pass.

In 1977, Bob led the NFL in touchdown passes.

48

Craig Morton

Orange Power

Somebody ought to make a movie about it. The opening scene would show Craig Morton in a New York Giant uniform. He is running onto the field and the fans are booing loudly. Craig barely notices. He's used to it. They booed him in 1975. Why shouldn't they boo him in 1976?

Then the scene switches to Boston. A 50-year-old man with red hair is sitting in his living room talking to his wife. He's six feet tall with a rugged, strong body; but, slumped in his chair, he looks small and tired. The man is Red Miller. He has been coaching football for 28 years. He has been an assistant coach for so long that he's just about given up hope of ever being the head coach of his own pro team. He and his wife are talking about the dream that will never be.

Now we go to Denver, Colorado, a mile-high city carved out of the Rocky Mountains. A city that is proud of its gold-rush history, proud of its craggy mountains, and proud of its football team, the Denver Broncos... even if the Broncos haven't won a division championship in their entire 17 years of existence. The camera moves to a man in the Denver Bronco offices. He picks up a phone. He places a call to Red Miller in Boston and offers Red the job as head coach of the Broncos. Miller lets out a yell. He hugs his wife. Suddenly, he looks seven feet tall.

Once he is settled in Denver, Miller sets out to find a quarterback — someone with a strong arm, someone with leadership qualities, someone with experience. The quarterback he chooses is Craig Morton.

The rest of the movie tells the extraordinary story of how three losers — Morton, Miller and the Denver fans — get together and become big winners. It is a true story. It all really happened.

When he came to Denver to play for Red Miller in 1977, Craig Morton was considered all washed up. He'd had a lot of athletic glory in his life, but not recently. And now it seemed too late for any more. He was, after all, 34 years old.

As a boy, Craig grew up in Campbell, California, not very far from San Francisco. His father, a glass blower, had once tried out for baseball's major leagues. Craig was a good baseball player, too. He was on his high

Craig Morton of the Denver Broncos. Bronco receiver Jack Dolbin says Craig "throws a very catchable ball, with a lot of smoke on it."

school team and earned all-state honors. He was also all-state in two other sports, basketball and football.

In college, at the University of California, his sport was football and his position was quarterback. Passing for 2,121 yards in his senior season alone, he was an All-America. Big and strong at 6-4 and 210 pounds, he was rated as an exceptional pro prospect.

Craig was the Dallas Cowboys' first-round draft choice in 1965. For four years he sat on the Cowboy bench as the number two quarterback behind Don Meredith. Craig figured to be on the bench again a fifth year, 1969. But, surprisingly, Meredith announced that even though he was still young, he was retiring from football.

Craig was off camping in northern California the day Meredith made that announcement. He didn't hear the news until much later. Craig was driving home from the camping trip when he turned on the car radio and learned what Meredith had done. Craig was surprised. He was delighted. He was now number one. He was so excited that he almost lost control of the car. "It's a miracle," he said later, "that there wasn't a string of wrecks along the highway."

Craig played well as the Cowboys' number one quarterback. He led the Cowboys to the Super Bowl in the 1970 season. But there was something wrong. The mix was wrong. Craig Morton and the Dallas Cowboys never quite blended together. Morton wasn't the kind of quarterback that coach Tom Landry liked. And Landry wasn't the kind of coach who could bring out the very best in Craig. Their personalities clashed. Landry was too serious and unbending for Craig. And Craig was too much of a fun-loving rebel for Landry.

So, Landry began alternating Craig and Roger Staubach at quarterback. Then, when Roger took over the position by himself in 1971, Craig was back on the bench. And in 1974 Dallas traded Craig to the New York Giants.

Craig spent two-and-a-half horrible years with the Giants. They were years filled with interceptions, fumbles, losses, and boos. The Giants were a weak team and Craig couldn't help them. "It wasn't fun in New York," he said one day. "The only thing I enjoyed was the restaurants and the Broadway plays. The football was all very frustrating."

The fans, the press, the professional football world gave up on Craig Morton. They figured he would fumble around for a year or two more and then just fade away.

That's when Red Miller came along. He was looking for an experienced quarterback to lead his Denver Broncos. "I always thought Morton had one of the best throwing actions I'd ever come across," Red explained. "He has that nice, high release, overhand, a strong arm, and a good touch for throwing." To be certain, Red watched movies of Craig's old Dallas games. He liked what he saw. And washed-up Craig Morton came to Denver.

Craig immediately proved that Red Miller had made a wise choice. "The first time Craig came into a huddle, he was in total charge," one of the Bronco receivers, Jack Dolbin, said admiringly. "He called the plays with complete confidence."

Not only did Craig impress the Broncos with his leadership, but he impressed them with his passing as well. "He throws a very catchable ball, with a lot of smoke on it," Dolbin said. "You can really feel it hit your hands."

When the season opened, Craig continued to play well. And the Broncos began to win. They won every one of their first six games. They were in first place and Craig was a big hero. What had happened to suddenly make him such a star? "I'm the same player," he said. "The situation is different."

He may have been the same player, but he sure looked different. One reporter wrote: "Like an old car, he has been restored. The dents pounded out. The chrome polished."

The man who did the pounding and polishing was Red Miller. And he didn't do it teaching Morton anything new. He did it by building up Craig's confidence. He did it by earning Craig's respect. He did it by showing trust. And it worked; because, unlike what had happened at Dallas, this time the mix was just right. Miller and Morton blended perfectly. "The man is a dream to play for," said Craig. "You do things his way, but you never lose your individuality."

Miller was tough but nice. He treated his team with respect. He could be very serious: "This is the way it's going to be; get used to it." And he could be fun: "Okay, men, time for a popsicle break."

He gave them firmness. He gave them freedom. And they gave him wins. With Craig at the helm, Miller molded a team with spirit and the will to win. They developed a togetherness that made them push themselves to do their very best — for Miller, for Morton, and for the third part of the combination, the Denver fans.

Craig had never seen anything like those fans. They had been intensely loyal all those losing years. Ever since 1971, Mile High Stadium had sold out every seat for every game. Now, finally, the Denver fans had a super team. And as Craig and the Broncos piled up more and more wins, the fans went wild.

The Broncos, who wore orange-red uniforms, called their defensive line the "Orange Crush." And the fans decided to go crazy over orange. Throughout Denver there were orange shirts, orange banners, orange scarves, orange buttons; radios were orange — and so were can openers, shower curtains, sweaters, Christmas trees. There were even some fans who dyed their hair orange!

The store shelves began emptying of anything orange. By the time the season was near its end, you coundn't buy a can of orange paint in the entire city of Denver. A company that made a drink called Orange Crush had to hire twenty more people in its factory in order to keep up with the demand.

One fan, who was in the building-wrecking business, had a job to tear down a 12-story building just before a game against Oakland. He painted the three-ton wrecking ball orange and he hung a huge sign on the building. The sign said "OAKLAND." As hundreds of fans cheered, the big orange ball crushed Oakland.

How could you not go out there and play harder than ever before in your life? If you're Craig Morton and you've just come from two years of being booed as a Giant, you'd want to do anything you could not to disappoint those fantastic fans.

He didn't disappoint them. He built win on top of win until he brought his team into the playoffs. Never before had the Denver Broncos been in the pro football championship playoffs. Now they were. And if they could get two playoff victories, the Denver Broncos would be in the Super Bowl.

Their first playoff game was against the Pittsburgh Steelers. Twice in the last three years these Steelers had won the Super Bowl, had been the champions of all pro football. Now, they wanted a third title. And they wanted it badly.

Morton is protected from the charging Oakland defense by teammates Lonnie Perrin (35), Andy Maurer (74), and Claudie Minor (71).

The Steelers fought hard against the Broncos. And the Broncos fought back. In the fourth quarter the score was tied, 21-21. The Broncos got the ball and Craig moved them to the Steeler 34-yard line. Jim Turner kicked a field goal and Denver led, 24-21.

A few moments later, Tom Jackson of the Broncos intercepted a pass. Denver had the ball again. Craig dropped back on third down and fired the ball into the end zone. His favorite receiver, Haven Moses, caught it. Touchdown. Denver was ahead, 30-21.

But no. The officials said the touchdown didn't count. They called a penalty. Movies would show that the officials were wrong, that Denver had done nothing to deserve a penalty. But that would be too late to change anything. So, even though the officials were wrong, Craig's touchdown pass didn't count.

The best Denver was able to get was another three-point field goal by Turner. So instead of leading 30-21, they led by only six points, 27-21. A Steeler touchdown and extra point would put Pittsburgh in the lead. And there were five minutes and ten seconds left in the game. Plenty of time for the Steelers to do it.

But soon Tom Jackson came through again. Another interception. Denver had the ball on Pittsburgh's 33-yard line. Craig ran on the field. He could play conservatively now — call safe running plays and hope that they would eat up the remaining time. Or he could gamble and try for a touchdown that would clinch the game.

On first down Craig called a running play. On second down, he decided to gamble. He went to the sidelines and told Miller that he wanted to try for a touchdown pass, that he wanted to throw a "bomb."

Miller was surprised. He didn't want to gamble. "Craig had to ask me twice," the coach said afterward. "But I've learned that they're the ones playing the game and lots of times their ideas are better than ours."

There it was. That trust between the quarterback and the coach. That perfect mix. Coach Miller gave Craig permission to gamble.

Craig faded behind his blockers. He looked downfield. Then he threw the ball toward the goal line 34 yards away. He aimed it for Jack Dolbin, the receiver who'd felt such confidence in Craig the very first time Craig took over in a Bronco huddle.

It was perfect pass. Dolbin caught it for a touchdown. And Denver had clinched the victory.

After the Steelers came the Oakland Raiders. The Steelers had won two of the past three Super Bowls. Oakland had won the third—the 1977 Super Bowl. The Raiders were pro football's defending champions. They were tough.

And not only were the Raiders tough to beat under any circumstances, but it looked as if the Broncos might have to play them without Craig. He was hurt. He had hurt his hip and was in the hospital.

Craig stayed in the hospital nearly all week before the Raider game. He couldn't throw even one pass in practice. Coach Miller said that until the minute the game started he wouldn't know if Craig would be able to play.

Craig was in great pain the day of the game. He could barely run. But he felt he had to try. Craig started the game. He "was limping noticeably as he dropped back for his first important pass of the game," *Newsweek*'s Pete Axthelm wrote "but somehow he peered through the pain, spotted a hole in the Oakland secondary—and hit Haven Moses with a touchdown bomb. Much later, when the Raiders seemed to be charging toward one of their familiar comeback victories, Morton's hip seemed to betray him entirely. He stumbled, righted himself and barely avoided an Oakland lineman. And then he coolly located Moses in the end zone and hit him with another touchdown pass. The Broncos held on to win, 20-17, and when it was over Morton fell to his knees in the locker room, allowing the pain and exhilaration to wash over him, thanking his teammates and God for the shining moment that had eluded him for so long."

Outside, in the Denver Stadium, those great fans were singing and laughing and cheering. Inside the locker room, Craig was slumped on the floor. "It's not the hip," he said. "I'm frankly just overcome with emotion."

The Broncos were the champions of the American Football Conference. And "the 34-year-old Morton," Axthelm wrote, "has emerged as the game's most striking symbol of courage, skill, and dignity."

It was hard to believe. No one had ever thought that the Broncos, led by a couple of washed-up men, could make it to the Super Bowl. But Craig had fooled them all. The Broncos went to New Orleans in January, 1978, about to play Super Bowl XII.

In New Orleans, on the morning of his first practice for the Super Bowl, Craig got up at six a.m. "I just sat alone for two hours thinking about it," he said later. "When my wife, Susie, and I were having breakfast, I said to her, 'Hey, you know we're going to the Super Bowl.' I'm just beginning to realize it, and I'm excited."

He had every right to be excited. He was the man who had put them there. Craig's season had been spectacular. He had quarterbacked Denver to two playoff victories. He had led the team to 12 wins and only two losses in the regular season. His passes had gained nearly 2,000 yards in the regular season alone. He had been intercepted only eight times. He was a hero. And here he was, facing his old team, the Dallas Cowboys, in the Super Bowl. He was in a contest with Roger Staubach, the man who had taken his job. It was a game Craig Morton wanted to win — very, very much.

If this were a make-believe movie, we could show Morton on the field — outthrowing, outscrambling, outplaying his old teammates. We could show the Broncos scoring, Miller cheering, the loyal fans wearing orange colors and screaming happily.

But that's not what really happened. In the first quarter of the game, Dallas jumped into a 10-0 lead and

Morton is blitzed by Dallas safety Randy Hughes. Craig was hurt on the play and had to leave the game.

never lost it. The final score of the game was Dallas 27, Denver 10.

The Broncos were outplayed. Perhaps part of the problem was that Morton's hip had been bothering him. perhaps Dallas won because it had so much more experience playing important games. Perhaps Dallas was simply the stronger, better team. Whatever the reason, the Miller-Morton-Denver fan combination didn't win the Super Bowl.

But even if they do make a movie about the way it really happened, it can still have a happy ending. Because Craig Morton was still a hero in Denver. He had had such a spectacular season, he had given so much pleasure to the fans, he had brought such excitement to the city, he had made such an inspiring comeback, that the words written by *Newsweek*'s Pete Axthelm still applied. Craig Morton, the man they thought was washed up, had indeed emerged as "the most striking symbol of courage" in the game.

Pro Football Passing Record of:
Craig Morton
Birthday: Feb. 5, 1943   Height: 6-4   Weight: 210
Team: Dallas Cowboys (1965-1974 [6 games])
New York Giants (1974 [8 games]-1976)
Denver Broncos (1977-   )

Year	Passes Thrown	Passes Completed	Percent	Average Gain	Total Yards	Touch-downs	Inter-ceptions
1965	34	17	50.0	5.09	173	2	4
1966	27	13	48.1	8.33	225	3	1
1967	137	69	50.4	7.14	978	10	10
1968	85	44	51.8	8.85	752	4	6
1969	302	162	53.6	8.67	2619	21	15
1970	207	102	49.3	8.79	1819	15	7
1971	143	78	54.5	7.91	1131	7	8
1972	339	185	54.6	7.07	2396	15	21
1973	32	13	40.6	5.44	174	3	1
1974	239	124	51.9	6.37	1522	9	13
1975	363	186	51.2	6.50	2359	11	16
1976	284	153	53.9	6.57	1865	9	20
1977	254	131	51.6	7.59	1929	14	8

In 1970, Craig led the NFL in average gain per pass.

Terry Bradshaw

Wonder Man with a Drawl

Pro football players are big men. Big and strong and tough. On the field they smash each other so furiously it sometimes seems as if they're made of steel. They are hard. They are heroes.

No wonder the fans forget. Forget that in most ways these big, tough men are the same as other people. They have the same feelings inside. And they can be hurt by words as well as by hard, physical knocks.

One day, in Pittsburgh, quarterback Terry Bradshaw was knocked flat on his back. Pain shot through his shoulder. He was in agony. Then he heard it. The cheer. The Pittsburgh fans were *cheering*. The Pittsburgh Steelers' quarterback was injured and in pain—and the fans in his hometown were happy about it.

"It's the most disgusting thing I've ever seen," said one of Terry's teammates.

Terry felt the hurt of the cheer even more than the hurt of the injury. He was a tall, powerful man — six feet, three inches and 225 pounds. But his huge body was no protection against the cruelty of the Pittsburgh fans.

The Steelers hadn't been playing well in the game, and the fans were taking it out on Terry. They were blaming him. Terry didn't know what to do.

Until he came to Pittsburgh, football fans had always loved Terry. They admired his skill as a runner and passer. And they really admired his courage.

Once, in a college all-star game, Terry was flattened so hard he broke two ribs. But he refused to leave the field. He stayed in the game for two more quarters and continued to fire hard, bullet passes.

Before another college all-star game, Terry ran too hard in practice. He pulled a muscle in his leg. The coach saw that Terry was in great pain. He told Terry to rest, not play in the game. But Terry said no. He played in the game anyway, and was a star.

Terry learned how to be a tough football player in Woodlawn, Louisiana. Woodlawn was a quiet, friendly community. Terry's dad, Bill Bradshaw, had settled in Woodlawn because he felt it was a perfect place for children to grow up.

Bill Bradshaw had run away from his own home in

Pittsburgh's Terry Bradshaw sweeps right end for 11 yards.

the Tennessee hills when he was 13 years old. He had then roamed the country, working at a lot of different jobs and going to a lot of different schools. When Bill had children of his own, he decided to give them the kind of home he wished he had had. A strict home — with rules and curfews and religion.

As a boy, Terry went to lots of religious meetings with his mother, and he thought about becoming a minister. He also practiced football every chance he got. "Can you guess how many passes I've thrown in my life?" he once asked a reporter. "There was a time when I threw passes every day. Ask my dad about the years I threw a football from morning to night."

Terry played quarterback in high school and then at Louisiana Tech — a small college that hardly anyone had heard of. Until Terry arrived.

During Terry's four years at Louisiana Tech, pro football scouts streamed to the college to watch him play. And they all came away talking about his arm.

"Best arm I ever saw," one scout said.

"Quickest delivery," said another.

"A real rifle arm!" said still another.

In Pittsburgh, Art Rooney, Jr., read the reports from the Steelers' scouts. Rooney was in charge of picking new players for the Steelers, and he became very interested in Terry. He watched movies of Terry playing. He went to Louisiana Tech and watched Terry throw in practice.

"What kind of guy is Bradshaw?" Rooney asked a student who was collecting footballs after practice and stuffing them into a sack.

"Wonderful guy," said the student.

Rooney asked more questions. With every answer, Rooney became more and more impressed. The student kept saying the most fantastic things about Terry.

Everything was so complimentary that Rooney finally said, "You sound like a relative."

The boy smiled proudly. "I'm his brother," said Gary Bradshaw.

In 1969, Terry's senior season at Louisiana Tech, the scouts were praising him as highly as his brother had. And almost every single National Football League team wanted him.

The Steelers got him. And their fans were very excited. In 1969, the Steelers had been the worst team in the NFL. But now they had a great quarterback.

The fans expected great things from Terry right away. But they forgot that he was young. They forgot that he was inexperienced. And they didn't have any patience. They got angry when Terry made mistakes.

Sometimes, Terry called poor plays. Once Terry became so nervous in the huddle that he couldn't call any play at all. The young quarterback just stared down at the ground, unable to speak. Finally someone else called the play.

The fans were disappointed. The fans were angry.

Terry gets good news: He was first pick in college draft. At Louisiana Tech he was known as a "rifle armed passer."

The fans were cruel. "Before I knew what hit me," Terry later remembered, "everyone was calling me a big, dumb kid who had a strong arm and not enough sense to come out of the rain. A hick. That's what they painted me as — a hick."

They called him "Li'l Abner," after the comic-strip character. Li'l Abner of the comics was big. So was Terry. Li'l Abner had a huge, square jaw. So did Terry. And Li'l Abner was dumb. So was Terry, according to the fans.

"Some things have been said about me that I hate," Terry said. "How would you like to be called stupid?"

Day after day, Terry grew unhappier. Once, after he was injured in a game, Terry stopped at a gas station. His right arm was in a sling. A group of teenagers recognized him and walked over to his car.

"I thought they were going to say something like, 'Hang in there,'" Terry said later. Instead, they insulted him and called him names.

"I was really hurting," Terry said. "I wanted to kill them."

But he didn't fight with them. He forced himself to ignore them.

Even though the fans weren't happy with him, Terry did help the Steelers improve. The team had won only one game in 1969. But now, with Terry at quarterback, they won five games in 1970 and six in 1971.

In 1972, Terry did even better. Lots better. He not

only ran superbly and completed a lot of passes, but he became a good leader, too. The Steelers won 11 games and made it into the championship playoffs.

Now they needed three more victories to become the champions of pro football. Two victories would put them in the Super Bowl. A third victory—in the Super Bowl—would make them the champs.

Terry played his heart out and led them to one victory. Then he spent a week in the hospital with the flu. He left the hospital to play in the next game, but he was weak. And the Steelers lost.

The next season he helped the Steelers get into the playoffs again. But this time they didn't make it to the Super Bowl either. And a lot of people were disappointed. They said that the Steelers now had one of the finest teams in pro football—and the only reason they weren't champions was because they didn't have a good quarterback.

The fans weren't the only people picking on Terry. One day, a young woman asked Terry if she could interview him for her television show. He agreed. And with the cameras shooting away, the first question she asked was:

"Terry, are you really that dumb?"

Once more, people were saying he was stupid. And Terry felt terrible. "I'm as sensitive as anyone else," he told a friend, "but the fans don't seem to realize that."

All through the spring and summer, Terry tried hard

Bradshaw breaks clear with the ball.

to forget the criticism. He tried to look ahead. He was determined to prove that people were wrong about him. "I'm going to have a good year," he said. "The best ever."

Terry still had his confidence. But now the Steeler coaches didn't have any confidence in Terry. When the 1974 season began, they took away his job. Another man, Joe Gilliam, became the Steelers' quarterback.

The Steelers started off the season well. But then they began to slip. They were a good football team, but they weren't playing like champions. They were missing something.

What they were missing was Terry Bradshaw. And toward the end of the season they gave him back his job. Now the Steelers started to roll. With Terry at quarterback, they made it into the playoffs for the third straight year. Once again, all they needed were three more victories to become the champions of pro football.

Terry got them the first victory; then he got them the second. And now, for the first time ever, the Steelers were in the Super Bowl.

Clearly, Terry had been the star of the first two playoff games. But all week before the 1975 Super Bowl, people kept asking him questions that hurt him inside. One reporter even asked him, flat out, the same question that had so terribly wounded him once before: "Terry, are you really that dumb?"

When the reporter did that, Terry told a friend later,

"I just walked away. You know, if we lose it's because I'm dumb. If we win it's because everyone played well and I got caught up in the action. At least, that's what everyone will say. People are funny. If you talk slow, you're dumb. If you talk fast, you're a sharpie. I'm sick of it. Even when I play well, they say I'm a dumbbell."

When the Super Bowl game began, Terry stopped worrying about what people thought about him or said about him. He had only one thing on his mind — winning. He called shrewd plays. He threw sharp passes. He ran hard and with speed.

One time, he tucked the ball under his arm and ran around end for 17 yards. A swarm of Minnesota Vikings finally pounced on him. The referee blew his whistle, calling an end to the play. But Terry was concentrating so hard on winning that he never even heard the whistle. He squirmed free and kept running. The extra yards didn't count, of course. But they showed everyone just how hard Terry was battling.

His runs gained 33 yards for the Steelers in the Super Bowl. And his passes gained another 96. He threw 14 passes in the game and completed nine of them. One of the passes, a stinging bullet, was caught for a touchdown.

All game Terry battled with every ounce of his courage and energy. And when it was over, the Steelers had won, 16-6. Their defense had been magnificent. Their running back, Franco Harris, had been magnificent, too. And so had their quarterback, Terry Bradshaw.

The next season, Terry did it again. He quarterbacked the Steelers to their second straight Super Bowl win. And now he had a new reputation. The quarterback they once called "dumb" was now known as a "super clutch player," as a man who played his best when it counted most.

After his first Super Bowl victory, Terry sat in the locker room and said, "I've looked at all sides now — being a hero and being a jerk." Today, he was a hero. And, finally, all of the Steeler fans loved him. Many of the same people who had once been so cruel to him were now out on the streets of Pittsburgh, in fact. And they were cheering wildly at every mention of Terry Bradshaw's name.

Pro Football Passing Record of:

Terence Paxton Bradshaw

Birthday: Sept 2, 1948 Height: 6-3 Weight: 225

Team: Pittsburgh Steelers (1970-   )

Nickname: Terry

Year	Passes Thrown	Passes Completed	Percent	Average Gain	Total Yards	Touch-downs	Inter-ceptions
1970	218	83	38.1	6.47	1410	6	24
1971	373	203	54.4	6.06	2259	13	22
1972	308	147	47.7	6.13	1887	12	12
1973	180	89	49.4	6.57	1183	10	15
1974	148	67	45.3	5.30	785	7	8
1975	286	165	57.7	7.19	2055	18	9
1976	192	92	47.9	6.13	1177	10	9
1977	314	162	51.6	8.04	2523	17	19

In 1977, Terry led the NFL in average gain per pass.

Jim Plunkett

Battling Back

Some kids have it easy. If they want a bike, they just ask for it. If they need money, they get an allowance. If they have to go somewhere, Mom or Dad drives them.

Jim Plunkett didn't grow up that way. Both his mother and father were blind.

Jim's father sold newspapers in restaurants and at the post office in San Jose, California. He didn't earn very much money and he needed all the help Jim could give. When the other kids were out playing, Jim was helping his father. As soon as he was old enough to carry a bundle of papers, Jim got himself a newspaper route. He pumped gas when he was 12 years old. He worked in a grocery store when he was a little older.

But somewhere, in between the jobs, Jim found time

to throw a football. In 1962, when he was 14, Jim entered a passing contest. When it was his turn to throw, Jim walked out onto the field, stepped into position, and released the ball. The officials stared, wide-eyed. Jim had flipped the football 63 yards.

When he got to high school, Jim naturally tried out for the football team. But the coach told him he was too fat to play football. So Jim joined the wrestling team. He worked hard. He did lots of exercises. And he grew strong. He turned those pounds of fat into pounds of muscle.

The next time he tried out for football, he made the team. And as a high-school quarterback, Jim was outstanding. Once a scout from a college watched as Jim played. Most of the time, scouts are pretty cool. They watch, they take notes, they say a few words to the coach. This scout couldn't hold himself down.

"Look at the ball!" the scout shouted. "Look at where the ball is! Right on the chest every time."

Jim earned a lot of good reports from the scouts and he received quite a few offers of college scholarships. He was a fine student as well as a fine football player. And he chose Stanford University, one of the best colleges in the country.

Jim was very happy. But soon he had a lot of things to worry about. The doctors at Stanford told him that he had a lump on his neck and needed an operation. He might never be able to play football again.

Plunkett looks for a receiver during a game with the Los Angeles Rams.

Jim was frightened. Football was important to him. He was counting on football as a way out—a way out of being poor. Football was giving him a chance to go to college. From there, Jim hoped he might make it into the pros. Football was the way Jim Plunkett had planned to care for his family.

Jim had an argument with the doctors. "No operation," he said. "No, I won't have it operated on."

But Jim's parents didn't agree with him. They knew that football was not everything. Football was not life. Football was an extra. Jim had the operation, and it turned out okay.

After the operation, Jim went back to football—too soon. He wasn't really healthy enough to play.

"I didn't play well," he later said. "In fact, I played crummy."

Jim also had trouble with his schoolwork. And he had trouble making friends. He felt uncomfortable at Stanford. There were so many rich students. They were so different from him. Both of Jim's parents were Mexican-American. There were very few students at Stanford with his background.

"What am I doing here?" he said to himself. "Maybe I'd better get out and do something else."

But Jim had come through harder times — and he decided that he was going to come through this, too.

The best way, he decided, was to move slowly and surely. He chose to sit out the next football season. He practiced with the team, building up his health, developing his arm and skills. But he didn't play in any games.

In 1968, Jim began his varsity career. He completed a lot of passes. He ran for touchdowns. He controlled the ball with skill and confidence. Suddenly, Stanford was a winning team.

The students with whom he had felt so uncomfortable were now cheering him. A new chant rang out from the stands:

"Plunkett to 'em! Plunkett to 'em! Plunkett to 'em!"

And his teammates, too, had a special feeling for Jim. One of them, whose job it was to protect Jim during pass rushes, said, "If anyone ever got by me and hurt Jim, I think I'd turn in my uniform."

Jim played sensational football for Stanford. An opposing coach said, "He has real strength and good speed. If you go all out to blitz him, he'll eat you alive."

And when Jim finished his last season, another opponent said, "I'm very happy to see him graduate."

In 1970, Jim was awarded the Heisman Trophy as the best college football player in the country. And he was on his way to the pros—to the New England Patriots in the National Football League.

The differences between pro football teams and college football teams are enormous. A lot of big college stars have crumbled in the pros. The training is harder. The games are rougher. The pressure is sometimes unbearable. There are hundreds of new plays to learn, new people to meet.

Plunkett first played pro ball with the New England Patriots. Here he's shown airborne, leaping through the air for a few extra yards.

Plunkett tries to scramble and is caught between Joe Campbell (73) and Elex Price (75) of the New Orleans Saints.

And, of course, the quarterback has the hardest job of all since he must be the team leader. There he is, coming onto a team of veterans, unsure of himself, nervous about being in the pros—and he has to be the leader.

Perhaps for Jim Plunkett it wasn't as hard as it was for some other young quarterbacks. He had never had it easy. He had always worked hard for what he wanted. And he was prepared to work hard again.

Still, Jim made a lot of mistakes his first year. It took him time to master all the complicated plays of the Patriots.

"What really bothered me was when I'd call a play in the huddle," he said when the season was over. "I'd say, 'Flanker 40...40...uh, no, I mean Flanker 30.' When you do that too often you worry that you're losing the team's confidence."

Another time, Jim huddled with his team. He called out a play, clapped his hands to say, "Okay, let's get to it," and everyone except Randy Vataha, who had played with Jim at Stanford, just stood there. They just stood there and stared.

"I'd called a Stanford play," Jim said later. "Vataha and me, we knew the play. The rest of them thought I'd gone crazy. I felt like crawling away."

But, of course, he stuck to it. And as the season went on, Jim improved. By the time the season ended, in fact, he had thrown 19 touchdown passes.

Joe Namath and Fran Tarkenton had thrown 18

touchdown passes when they were rookies. Bob Griese had thrown 15. Johnny Unitas had thrown only nine. But Jim had thrown 19.

"Plunkett is going to be a superstar," said Deacon Jones, who had been an all-star pass rusher for many years. "And he'll get there faster than any quarterback who has come up in my time."

Before Jim joined them, the Patriots were a terrible team. They still weren't a very good team, but now they weren't pushed around as easily as they had been in the past. Opponents respected Jim. They knew that every time he faded back, he had the ability to throw for a touchdown. They had to be very careful to cover the pass receivers tightly.

In Jim's next season, 1972, the Patriots still weren't a strong team. But they were showing signs of getting better. And a man named Bob Waterfield, who had once been an All-Pro quarterback himself, said, "If I was going to start a pro team tomorrow, and could choose any young quarterback in the world, I'd take Jim Plunkett."

Jim was a big fellow — six feet, three inches and 215 pounds. He had always been able to fire a football long distances, but now his accuracy was improving, too. And so was his play-calling. He was developing the knack of fooling opponents with his plays.

And he was becoming famous. A lot of people were writing stories about him in newspapers and magazines. And people always wanted to know what it had been like growing up as the son of parents who were blind.

Jim didn't want people to think he was special. He didn't want people to feel sorry for him. "I always got a lot of support from both my parents," he told them. "It wasn't until later, looking back, that I found anything unusual in having blind parents. When I was growing up, that was just how it was at home."

During the 1973 season, Jim and the New England Patriots continued to get better. And in 1974 they were ready. They opened the season against the Miami Dolphins. The Dolphins had won the Super Bowl for two straight years. But the Patriots beat them. With Jim throwing pinpoint passes, the Patriots beat the champs.

Next, they beat the New York Giants. Then they beat the Los Angeles Rams. And after that they destroyed the Baltimore Colts, 42-3. The Patriots had played four games — and won them all. And Jim had thrown nine touchdown passes.

The Patriots were suddenly a team with a chance to win a championship. Jim continued to throw great passes and the team continued to win.

Halfway through the season, though, some important players got hurt. Jim still played well, but he didn't have as much help as before. And, of course, he couldn't do it alone.

Still, the Patriots kept trying. And they just missed getting into the playoffs. The team that had been so terrible four years earlier was now one of the best in the league.

The next season Jim was injured. He played in only five games. The Patriots weren't sure he would be able to get back in tough shape again. So they traded him to a team willing to take a chance, the San Francisco 49ers. The 49ers gave up a lot to get Jim. But they were confident he would work hard and make a big comeback.

Jim had some rough times during his first season with the 49ers. But, as always, he worked long and hard to get back in the groove. And by the end of his second season as a 49er, he suddenly began playing with his old superstar flair. Against the Dallas Cowboys on December 12, 1977, in fact, he had one of his greatest games ever. He completed 15 passes for 263 yards. Three of those passes were for touchdowns.

San Francisco fans began looking to the future. Many of them had been following Jim's career since his young days in nearby San Jose. They knew how much he could do to help a team win big. And he had just shown them he still had it.

A few months after the 1977 season, the 49ers announced a new trade. Another player who grew up in the San Francisco area was coming home to play for the 49ers. And that player was O.J. Simpson, the greatest running back in the game. The 49ers had just acquired him from the Buffalo Bills.

Now, the football fans in San Francisco were really

excited. Indeed, with O.J. running for them and Jim Plunkett passing, the 49ers' future looked really bright.

Pro Football Passing Record of:

James William Plunkett, Jr.

Birthday: Dec 5, 1947   Height: 6-3   Weight: 215

Team: New England Patriots (1971-1975)

San Francisco 49ers (1976-   )

Nickname: Jim

Year	Passes Thrown	Passes Completed	Percent	Average Gain	Total Yards	Touch-downs	Inter-ceptions
1971	328	158	48.2	6.58	2158	19	16
1972	355	169	47.6	6.19	2196	8	25
1973	376	193	51.3	6.78	2550	13	17
1974	352	173	49.1	6.98	2457	19	22
1975	92	36	39.1	6.21	571	3	7
1976	243	126	51.9	6.55	1592	13	16
1977	248	128	51.6	6.83	1693	9	14

Bert Jones

Strong-Armed Country Boy

It isn't easy to be a four-year-old kid in leg braces. Everyone else is running, playing ball, laughing. And you can't because you've got this disease called "rickets" that you don't even understand. They tell you it has to do with your bones. But all you know is that they strapped your legs into these metal things and took you away from the fun.

That's what happened to four-year-old Bert Jones. For two years he stumbled around in his braces. The other kids played ball. Bert watched. The other kids ran. Bert watched. The other kids rode their bikes. Bert watched.

But one day the watching was over. The braces came off, and Bert took off like a race horse at the starting gate. For him, games weren't just games. They were serious business to a kid who hadn't been able to play for two years.

From the minute the braces came off, Bert set out to prove himself. It didn't matter what the game was. Bert wanted to win.

"Whatever Bert tried," his father remembered years later, "he wouldn't stop until he was the best. It didn't matter if it was marbles, horseshoes, or tossing rocks. Bert couldn't even swing on the swings without yelling to the kid next to him, 'Bet I can swing higher than you can.' "

Of all the games he played, football was Bert's favorite. Football was important to his whole family. Bert's father, Dub Jones, was a professional player, a halfback for the Cleveland Browns. In 1951, when Bert was wearing diapers, his father scored six touchdowns against the Chicago Bears, a record still standing in 1978. In the 1960's, when Bert was in his teens, he himself spent four summers at the Browns' training camp. Bert cleaned shoes, washed uniforms, and caught passes when the quarterbacks warmed up, picking up pointers whenever he could.

Bert grew strong and strapping and filled out to six feet, three inches and 212 pounds. He became a pro quarterback himself—for the Baltmore Colts. He took over the position once held by the most famous Baltimore Colt ever, Johnny Unitas. And people said that he was just like Johnny—a man with a great arm, brains, and coolness under pressure. A fierce competitor who knows how to win.

Bert Jones of the Baltimore Colts. Roger Carr once commented, " . . . this guy can unload one [pass for] 70 yards, anytime he likes and hit a dime."

But they didn't say those things right away. Bert didn't just walk in and become an instant pro football hero. Even though he had been a star quarterback in high school and an All-America quarterback at Louisiana State University, he still had a lot to learn. Even though he had spent many years of his youth around pro football players, he wasn't yet ready to actually take command of a pro team. He needed guidance. He had natural physical talent, but that alone is not enough for success in the tough, complicated pro game. Bert, who is a country boy from Ruston, Louisiana, once explained the problem this way: "It's easy to be a pumpkin, but you're not a jack-o'-lantern until you're cut."

Bert joined the Colts in 1973. He sat on the bench most of the 1973 season and much of the 1974 season, watching the Colts play very poorly. The team won only six games in both those seasons combined. And lost 22.

In 1975 a man named Ted Marchibroda took over as coach of the Colts. Marchibroda decided that Bert was the key to the Colts' future. So the coach spent night after night teaching the young quarterback how to beat defenses, telling him what to do in different situations. Bert listened and learned.

A lot of the other players on the Colts were young and inexperienced too. And they also learned a lot from the new coach. "Lumber," Bert once said. "We were like a lot of lumber. And Marchibroda was a carpenter. You can't throw a load of lumber on a lot and expect a house to go up by itself. It has to be built. And Marchibroda did the building."

But even a great carpenter can't do much with bad wood. And everyone knows you can't carve a rotten pumpkin. Bert Jones had to have something going in.

One thing he had was a strong, accurate arm. Back in 1974, even before Marchibroda took over, Bert had demonstrated that by completing 17 passes in a row against the New York Jets. Roger Carr, Bert's favorite receiver, told one reporter, "Hey, this guy can unload one 70 yards anytime he likes and hit a dime."

Even as a little kid in braces, Bert had had a strong arm. He used to show it off by throwing rocks. "Best rock thrower in Lincoln County, Louisiana," according to his dad. "And if you can flang a rock real good, you can flang anything."

As a boy, Bert learned to throw baseballs, too. "In the beginning," Bert has said, "I was a Little League baseball pitcher with a strong arm and I think I learned to throw the football from throwing the baseball. Football was always my first love, but I've got to credit baseball for developing the arm."

A good, strong arm is only part of what is needed for good passing. "The real secret," said Bert, "is simple. You've gotta throw to the right people. You don't throw to somebody who is covered. An interception is a

Jones is caught behind the line of scrimmage by New England Patriot Richard Bishop.

mental error. It may not have been a bad throw, but it's a bad pass if it's thrown to the wrong place, or if it's thrown at the wrong time."

Sounds easy. It isn't. In order to recognize "the wrong place" or anticipate "the wrong time," a quarterback has to do a lot of homework. He has to watch movies of his future opponents' past games, looking for clues that will reveal what plays will work best against them. He has to spend a lot of time at practice, learning how to work perfectly with his own teammates so that every move will be smooth, precise. Success in a game is built upon precision in practice. A quarterback's success is built upon hours of throwing passes to receivers, handing off the ball to runners, taking snaps from the center, working on timing with guards and tackles, and studying opponents' defenses. "I play 90 percent of the game before it ever starts," Bert has said. "And if I'm gonna win, that's the way it has to be. I couldn't tell you I spend 40 hours a week on football, or 60 or 80. When I'm not actually working on it, I'm thinking about it all the time."

Bert was 23 years old when he began learning all this from Marchibroda in the summer of 1975. He worked hard. "I've never known a quarterback to put so much of his time into preparing himself mentally," Marchibroda said. "He takes films home every night."

When the 1975 season opened, fans did not expect much from the Colts. After all, the team had won only two games in all of 1974. But coach Marchibroda did. He had confidence in his team and in his young quarterback. He expected to win.

The Colts did win their first game. Then they lost four in a row. The fans weren't surprised. But then the Colts began to move. Against the New York Jets, Bert threw one touchdown pass for 89 yards and another for 90. The Colts won. The week after that, against his father's old team, the Cleveland Browns, Bert completed 16 of 26 passes for 153 yards and two touchdowns. He also led the Colts in running with 49 yards in four carries; and his team had another victory. Next, they played the Buffalo Bills. A few weeks earlier, Buffalo had beaten the Colts. Now, Buffalo took a 21-0 lead in the second period, and the Colts looked like losers again. But Bert refused to give up. He had studied the films and had spotted weaknesses in the Buffalo defense. And he began to take advantage of them. Coolly, confidently, the tall young quarterback began completing passes. And the Colts began to catch up. With Bert firing precision passes and halfback Lydell Mitchell running for big gains, Baltimore won, 42-35.

"It's only Bert's third NFL season," coach Marchibroda said. "But he's handling himself like an experienced quarterback. He's playing like a 30-year-old. We all knew he had potential, but he's taken it far beyond that. You can see some young players come into the league and make some progress, then never really emerge the way you thought they might. People can never say that about Bert."

The Colts beat the Jets again. Then they played the Miami Dolphins, who had won two of the last three Super Bowls, and beat them too. Baltimore beat Kansas City and the New York Giants. With Bert completing 23 passes for 232 yards, Baltimore beat Miami once more. Then, Baltimore beat the New England Patriots. The Colts had won nine straight games and were champions of the Eastern Division of the American Football Conference. They were in the playoffs.

In the playoffs, Baltimore met the Pittsburgh Steelers. Bert was hurt early in the game and the Colts lost. But what a season it had been. They had gone from last place in their division to first. People were calling them "the miracle Colts" and were calling Ted Marchibroda "the miracle coach." And they were calling Bert the best kid quarterback in the game.

The next season the kid became a man. Almost overnight. During training camp and the exhibition season, the Colts' owner, Robert Irsay, and the Colts' general manager, Joe Thomas, decided they weren't happy with the way Marchibroda was now coaching. They began criticizing the coach and telling him to do things differently. They criticized and criticized. Marchibroda said that their interference was preventing him from doing the best job possible, and he quit.

The players couldn't believe it. In one season Mar-

Bert Jones in action. The Associated Press named Jones the Most Valuable Player in the NFL and the Offensive Player of the Year in 1976.

chibroda had taken them from last place to first. And now he was gone because the owner and general manager didn't like the way he coached. Unbelievable.

The players held a meeting. "At the start of the meeting, there were five or six guys talking," defensive back Bruce Laird said later. "Then Bert took the whole thing over. It was as if he were saying, 'Hey, I'm not a kid anymore. I'll take care of this situation. You go home, keep your mouths shut, and I'll do the talking for you. Don't anybody say anything. I'm the leader. Let me handle it.'"

The next day, while his teammates kept quiet, Bert met with reporters and publicly criticized the owner and general manager. He said the Colts had to get Marchibroda back and that fans shouldn't go to any Colt games until that happened. After that, Bert called Pete Rozelle, the commissioner of the National Football League, and asked him to help. Then Bert met with Joe Thomas and told the general manager that the players wanted Marchibroda to come back. Thomas gave in. He promised to stay out of Marchibroda's way if the coach would return. Marchibroda came back. And Bert, who had been the team leader on the field, had now shown he was their leader off the field as well.

"I wasn't any kind of hero," he said. "It was just my place and my duty to do what I did. Most of the players couldn't afford to take a public stand. It could cost them their jobs, their means of support for their families. But I knew I could be the spokesman because I was in a financially secure position to speak up, and if I didn't play in Baltimore I could play someplace else."

Then it was time to play football. And once more, Bert led the Colts to a great season. In 1975 he had taken them to a 10-4 record. In 1976 he did even better. He passed for 3,104 yards, led them to an 11-3 record, which was the best in their division, and he was picked as the Most Valuable Player in the American Football Conference. Then in 1977 he was a superstar again. Passing for 2,686 yards, he led the Colts to their third straight championship in the AFC Eastern Division. The pumpkin clearly had been carved into a beautiful jack-o'-lantern.

After three great seasons, Bert was enjoying life in what he described as his "ole country-boy style." As part of his "ole country-boy style," he drove a red-and-white pickup truck, wore blue jeans and cowboy boots, and loved "to go huntin'." One day he telephoned a reporter who wanted to interview him. "Listen now," said Bert. "It's 4:30 in the mornin'. I'll be out front of your motel at five o'clock on the button. You better be there."

The reporter was there. And so was Bert, in jeans with red-and-white suspenders, a green hat, and a big smile. "We're goin' goosin'," Bert said. And with country music blasting on the radio of his pickup truck, Bert drove off with the reporter to hunt for geese. Two hours later, Bert had brought down three geese. "His

Jones is the victim of an "orange crush" by Denver Bronco defender, Lyle Alzado.

eye was as good with the shotgun," said the reporter, "as it is with the football."

For transportation, Bert not only drove a pickup truck, but also flew his own airplane — a twin-engine, six-seater Beechcraft Baron 58. He bought the plane when he was dating Danni Dupuis, the woman who became his wife after the '76 season. Danni lived a five-hour car ride away from Bert and, because of the distance, he couldn't see her as often as he wanted. So he went out and bought an airplane. With the plane, Bert was able to make the trip in only an hour.

For the wedding, "country boy" Bert, who has always hated to dress up, gave in to his family and went the whole proper way — fancy wedding, fancy clothes, fancy new shoes. But then, at the last minute, when no one was looking, Bert took off the new shoes and put on his comfortable old cowboy boots. "I shined them up so no one would notice," he said later. "And no one did notice—until I kneeled at the altar. There were holes in both soles!"

After they were married, Bert and Danni moved into a house across the street from the one his parents lived in. "We've always been a close family," Bert said. Especially Bert and his father. "He's a good man," Bert said. "Patient, nice, and just. I always wanted to be like him. That's one reason I knew I would play pro ball."

That was a mighty big ambition for a little kid in leg braces. But he was willing to work for it — and his efforts certainly paid off in the end.

Pro Football Passing Record of:

Bertram Hays Jones

Birthday: Sept. 7, 1951   Height: 6-3   Weight: 212

Team: Baltimore Colts (1973-   )

Nickname: Bert

Year	Passes Thrown	Passes Completed	Percent	Average Gain	Total Yards	Touch-downs	Inter-ceptions
1973	108	43	39.8	4.99	539	4	12
1974	270	143	53.0	5.96	1610	8	12
1975	344	203	59.0	7.22	2483	18	8
1976	343	207	60.3	9.05	3104	24	9
1977	393	224	57.0	6.83	2686	17	11

In 1976, Bert led the NFL in total yards gained passing.

In 1977, Bert led the NFL in passes completed.

Fran Tarkenton

Veteran Scrambler

The bubblegum cards were all set up on the bed. Each one had a picture of a pro football player. There were many cards, but the ones 10-year-old Fran Tarkenton liked best had pictures of the Philadelphia Eagles.

He looked down at a card with a picture of Steve Van Buren, the Eagles' great runner. Then he looked at another with a picture of Pete Pihos, the huge, strong end. These were the players who, a year earlier in 1949, had led the Eagles to the National Football League championship.

Fran was getting ready to play a special game with the cards. It was a game he had made up. He would take the cards of men from two different teams and have them play each other. He had his own way of making them block and tackle, run and pass.

This day the Eagles would be playing the Washington Redskins. Fran picked up Van Buren's card. "Steve," he said, "we're going to be running you wide a lot today."

In his mind, Fran imagined Van Buren's answer: "Great, Coach."

Then Fran talked with other players. He asked how they were feeling. He told them what he wanted them to do in the game. He worked out strategy.

Fran started the game. He moved the cards all over the bed, running football plays. And when the game was over, the undefeated bubblegum Eagles had won again.

Years later, Fran remembered those games. "I'd come home from school and run off those games till suppertime," he said. "And then after supper I'd do it the rest of the evening. While the other kids were doing homework I was wondering how to use Pete Pihos this week. This was my interest; this was my life."

Fran didn't play all his games on the bed. At the age of 10 he was also playing end for a boys' club football team in Washington, D.C. Later, when his family moved to Athens, Georgia, he played quarterback on the Athens YMCA team. He was able then to make good use of the football knowledge he had developed while running plays for the bubblegum teams.

Fran became the quarterback on his high-school team. He played so well he was picked as Georgia's

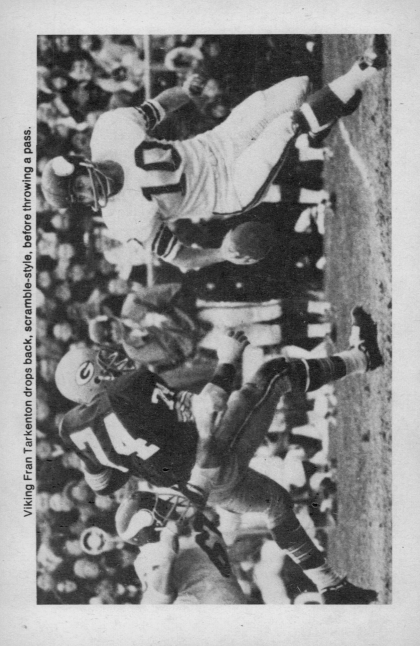

Viking Fran Tarkenton drops back, scramble-style, before throwing a pass.

All-State high-school quarterback. And he won a scholarship to the University of Georgia.

In his senior year at Georgia, Fran was one of the top quarterbacks in the country. He led his team to a 9-1 record and then went on to the pros, joining the Minnesota Vikings in 1961.

The Vikings were not a good team then, and they were happy to have a quarterback who had proved himself a winner. In fact, they knew that Fran simply hated to lose. "Show me a *good* loser," he had once said, "and I'll show you a *loser*."

Fran had learned about losing when he was a little boy, and he hadn't liked it. His older brother, Dallas, used to beat him at every sport. Dallas was bigger and stronger than Fran. He hit a baseball better, he ran faster, he threw a football farther.

One day Fran was so angry at losing to Dallas in a game that he ran into the kitchen and grabbed a butcher's knife. Fran chased his brother through the streets of Athens. For the first time ever, Dallas was afraid of Fran.

Fran, of course, was punished by his parents. And when he became a pro quarterback, Fran clearly remembered that horrible knife chase. "I still can't stand to lose," he said, "but I think I learned something from that experience. I didn't know it then, but I came to realize that losing my temper wouldn't get me anywhere. I think it's harder to have self-confidence than not to, and I work on keeping my cool."

In his very first game with the Vikings, Fran was not a loser. Far from it. He threw four touchdown passes and ran for a fifth touchdown. It was the opening game of the season and rookie quarterback Tarkenton had beaten the Chicago Bears, 37-13.

But then the Vikings lost seven games in a row. And they finished that 1961 season with a 3-11 record. Fran was miserable.

The next year was worse. They won only two games, and Fran learned what it was like to get booed.

The first time he heard the boos, he couldn't believe it. He had never been booed before. And not only were people booing him, they were yelling, too. They were yelling, "Get him out of there."

Norm Van Brocklin, the Viking coach, signaled Fran out of the game. As Fran walked off the field, a roar of cheers swept through the stadium. The Viking fans were cheering because Fran was leaving. He wanted to run somewhere and hide.

When Fran got to the sideline, a veteran on the team came over and put his arm around the young quarterback's shoulders.

"Well, kid," he said, "you've arrived! You're now an NFL quarterback. They've booed you and you've been replaced. Welcome to the club."

There were plenty of boos to come. Fran hated them — but they were part of pro football. And he knew that any pro player who couldn't learn to handle the pressure had better get out of the game.

During his next four years with the Vikings, Fran learned how to handle the pressure. And he learned a lot more besides. One of the very first things a pro quarterback has to learn, according to Fran, is to hold his temper and be nice to pass rushers. When a quarterback goes back to pass, it's the job of the pass rushers to smash into him before he lets the ball go. It's no fun to feel the weight of a 245-pound giant smashing into you — and the last thing that a quarterback wants is to get that giant angry by calling him names or insulting him.

"If you go out of your way to get them mad," Fran once said, "you're asking for more trouble. I don't want them to think that they're disturbing my afternoon one bit. So when they knock me down, I usually say something like, 'Good play, nice going!' My slogan is: Always leave 'em smiling."

Another thing Fran learned was how important it is to call out the signals loudly.

"When you lean over that center and start your count," he said, "you can't do it in cracking, timid voice. You can't stumble around. The simple truth is that the good quarterback has to be a loud mouth. He has to be heard all the way from the flankerback on the right to the split end on the left, and that's a distance of 25 or 30 yards.

"And he also has to call those signals clearly. If he wants to call out a signal using the words 'four-right-twenty-nine,' a quarterback has to make sure that every sound is pronounced perfectly. You've got to say, 'Four Right Twenty-Nine,' " Fran explained, "not, 'Foe Rat Twinny-Nan.' That's how a lot of plays are busted. There's no room for the least misunderstanding."

Fran was able to learn all those things. But he was never able to learn how to live happily with his coach, Norm Van Brocklin. Norm had been a great pro quarterback himself. But he had played with a different style than Fran's. Norm always took the snap from center, ran backwards in a straight line, stopped, and picked out his pass receivers. If they were covered by the defense, he would either throw the ball out of everybody's reach or he would allow himself to be tackled, which is called "eating the ball." Norm was a slow runner and he almost never tried to run with the ball. He was the kind of quarterback who is known as "a drop-back passer."

Fran, however, was a good runner. He would take the snap, go back and, if no receiver was free, he would run back and forth behind the line of scrimmage, dodging tacklers and hoping someone would get free for a pass. His scrambling style was exciting. People even gave Fran the nickname "Scrambler."

In his six years with the Vikings, Fran's great skill as a runner, passer, and leader had earned him a rating as one of the three or four top quarterbacks in pro football. But Van Brocklin hated the scrambling style, and always criticized him. Finally, Fran decided that he and the coach would just never be able to get along. Fran asked to be traded.

The Vikings traded him to the New York Giants. When he reported to the Giants in 1967, Fran quickly saw why they had finished last in the league with a 1-12-1 record in 1966. "I found it hard to believe that this was a National Football League team," Fran has written. "I had never seen worse playing personnel on any team, anywhere. When I got back to my room at night, I had an overwhelming desire to sit down and cry."

With Fran at quarterback, however, the Giants instantly improved. He led them to a 7-7 record in his very first season. Three years later, he brought them into their next-to-last game of the season with a chance to win the championship of their division.

In that game, the Giants played the St. Louis Cardinals. The Cardinals were tied for first place with the Dallas Cowboys. The Giants were right behind them. All week the Cardinals had been saying they would maul New York. At a big banquet in St. Louis, in fact, the Cardinals' defensive back, Larry Wilson, had stood in front of a cheering audience and shouted, "Let's stick the ball in Fran Tarkenton's ear!"

The day of the game, when the Giants ran on the field in St. Louis, "every seat," according to Fran, "seemed filled with a screaming, hooting Giant hater. They booed so loudly when we appeared that half of 'The Star-Spangled Banner' was drowned out by the noise."

But almost immediately, Fran quieted them down. The first time New York got the ball, he led the team to a touchdown. He kept scrambling around, a relatively small man of six feet and 190 pounds, dodging the huge pass rushers. He threw perfect passes. He called brilliant plays. And at the end of the game, when he took off his helmet, there was dirt in his short brown hair and a big smile on his youthful, handsome face. The Giants had won, 34-17. The Giants were now tied with the Cowboys for first place.

The Giants lost to the Los Angeles Rams the next week, and the Cowboys won the championship. But it had been a great season anyway. And Fran was chosen to play quarterback on the National Football Conference team in the Pro Bowl.

Fran was happy in New York. He was a popular hero, very much respected for his deep religious beliefs and for his participation in the Fellowship of Christian Athletes, a group of sports stars who work with young people. He was making a lot of money playing football for the Giants and working at various businesses in Atlanta, Georgia, where he lived when the football season ended.

But the next year the Giants didn't do very well. And as much as he loved New York, Fran began to wonder if he'd ever get a chance to play in a Super Bowl with the

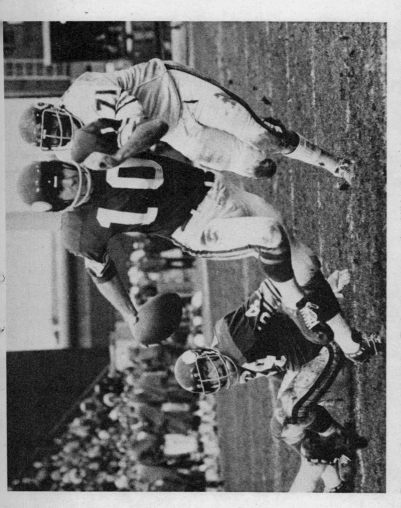

Fran the Scrambler in action. Tarkenton returned to Vikings, after 6 years with New York Giants, to lead Minnesota twice to Super Bowl.

Giants. More than almost anything, he wanted to lead a team to the Super Bowl.

Back in Minnesota, meantime, the Vikings had built up a team that had a very good chance of making it to the Super Bowl. The Vikings had played in one Super Bowl, in fact, a few years after Fran had left them. But the Vikings had Joe Kapp at quarterback when they went to that Super Bowl, and now Kapp was no longer on the team. The Vikings knew that they could not get another Super Bowl until they got a good quarterback. And the quarterback they wanted was Fran Tarkenton.

Coach Van Brocklin had left the Vikings the same year Fran had. So there was no reason why Fran wouldn't play for them. And when the Vikings made a trade with the Giants and brought him back to Minnesota, Fran was delighted. Now he had a chance to get to the Super Bowl.

The Viking fans were delighted, too. They didn't boo Fran any more, not even when he made mistakes. And in 1973, his second season back in Minnesota, Fran paid them back for their cheers by leading the Vikings to the Super Bowl.

The Vikings lost to Miami in that Super Bowl game. The very next year Fran took them to the Super Bowl again, and they were beaten by the Pittsburgh Steelers. In the 1976 season, he got them to the Super Bowl still another time, and they lost to Ken Stabler and the

Pro Football Passing Record of:

Francis Asbury Tarkenton

Birthday: Feb. 3, 1940   Height: 6-0   Weight: 190

Team: Minnesota Vikings (1961-1966)

New York Giants (1967-1971)

Minnesota Vikings (1972-   )

Nickname: Fran, Scrambler

Year	Passes Thrown	Passes Completed	Percent	Average Gain	Total Yards	Touch-downs	Inter-ceptions
1961	280	157	56.1	7.13	1997	18	17
1962	329	163	49.5	7.89	2595	22	25
1963	297	170	57.2	7.78	2311	15	15
1964	306	171	55.9	8.19	2506	22	11
1965	329	171	52.0	7.93	2609	19	11
1966	358	192	53.6	7.15	2561	17	16
1967	377	204	54.1	8.19	3088	29	19
1968	337	182	54.0	7.58	2555	21	12
1969	409	220	53.8	7.13	2918	23	8
1970	389	219	56.3	7.14	2777	19	12
1971	386	226	58.5	6.65	2567	11	21
1972	378	215	56.9	7.01	2651	18	13
1973	274	169	61.7	7.71	2113	15	7
1974	351	199	56.7	7.40	2598	17	12
1975	425	273	64.2	7.04	2994	25	13
1976	412	255	61.9	7.19	2961	17	8
1977	258	155	60.1	6.72	1734	9	14

Oakland Raiders. In 1977, Fran was having another fine year, but with five games remaining, he was injured and missed the rest of the season.

He was 37 years old, had played pro quarterback for 17 seasons, and said he thought it was time to retire. But then he changed his mind and decided to play in 1978. And whether or not he would ever get that Super Bowl victory he'd been dreaming of, the boy who had once played the game with bubblegum cards had proved beyond a doubt that he ranked among the greatest quarterbacks ever to compete on a professional football field.

In 1975 and 1976, Fran led the NFL in completed passes.

In 1975, Fran tied for the NFL lead in touchdown passes.

In 1977, Fran led the NFL in percent of passes completed.